Bristol Radical Pamph

Trouble on the Trams

Rob Whitfield

ISBN 978-1-911522-73-7

Bristol Radical History Group. 2024.
www.brh.org.uk
brh@brh.org.uk

In honour of the many Bristol Tramways' employees who, over 35 years, fought for and eventually won the right to belong to a trade union. Cheers drive!

Old Market, Bristol in about 1908.

Introduction

On 27th July 1901, the Bristol Tramways and Carriage Company dismissed 93 employees who had recently joined the National Union of Gas Workers and General Labourers. This was the start of a bitter dispute between the union and the company which lasted for several weeks, a struggle in which the wider trade union movement in Bristol rallied to the side of the tramwaymen.

The Bristol Tramways and Carriage Company

Horse-drawn trams were first introduced in Bristol in 1874, operated by the Bristol Tramways Company under licence from the City Corporation. In 1887 the company gained a monopoly on cab services from Temple Meads station and changed its name to the Bristol Tramways and Carriage Company Ltd. In 1895 Bristol became the first city in the country to see the introduction of electric trams. The first electrified line operated from Old Market St. to Kingswood. Lines to Eastville and Staple Hill, to Brislington, Knowle, Bedminster Down, Horfield, the Downs and to Hanham were completed in the next five years. By 1900, therefore, Bristol had an extensive network of tram lines. The Company employed around 1,200 people; it had its own electricity generating station at Counterslip near Bristol's city centre, a large depot with workshops at Brislington and smaller depots at the end of each line. In 1901 the number of passenger journeys on the tramway system totalled over thirty-six and a half million, placing it at the heart of the economic, social and cultural life of the city. With its monopoly position in the public transport system of Bristol, the company had become a highly successful enterprise.[1]

From the perspective of the directors and shareholders, the Tramways Company was very successful in generating profits. From gross receipts of £213,967, the Directors' Report for 1901 showed a profit of £70,382. Wages paid to employees in that year amounted to £71,360, barely more than total profits, whilst dividends paid to shareholders totalled £52,680. Very little of the profit was reinvested in the business or put into a reserve fund. As good as these results were for directors and shareholders, the company chairman, referring to the lock-out and strike during the summer of 1901, bemoaned the fact that the results

---

1 *The People's Carriage, 1874-1974*, Bristol Omnibus Company, Bristol, 1974.

"would have been more favourable but for the one untoward episode", going on to say that "during the few weeks of public excitement, the abnormal circumstances entailed some loss of traffic and special expenditure".[2]

The Tramways Company considered itself to be an enlightened employer. It claimed to have recently introduced a 10-hour working day and to be paying wages which were comparable to average pay in the city. A driver was paid about £1/4s per week and a conductor about 14s per week.[3] They also pointed to the provision of sick pay and funeral benefits out of the company's Provident Fund, and a pension fund which was in the process of being established, as evidence of their benevolence towards their employees. According to the union, however, there were numerous flaws in the company's claim to be a model employer. Overtime was a normal requirement, bringing the average working day up to 11½ or even 12 hours per day. New staff were placed on a 'spare staff' list and could be left with no paid work on some days, yet they were not allowed to take on other work. Deductions were made from wages into the Provident Fund but there was no refund of these contributions if a man's employment was terminated. Deductions from conductors' wages were also made if the figures for tickets issued and total takings did not tally.[4] These conditions led many tramways employees to join the union.

Nevertheless, in a company statement published in the local press on 1st August, Samuel White, its Managing Director asserted that the "company's employees have no grievance of any kind whatever".[5] "Service in this company," he went on, "has always borne an attractive reputation and, in future as hitherto, the company know that there will always be far more applicants for employment than there are places to be filled". In the eyes of the company directors, the dispute with the union was a "movement engendered by men outside the company's employ who have not hesitated to state that their organisation is a fighting one". From the outset, therefore, this was a struggle between a company which was determined to resist all attempts to unionise the workforce, and thereby allow 'outsiders' to upset their happy equilibrium, and a section of that workforce who believed that only with union support could they achieve

2 Bristol Tramways and Carriage Co. Ltd Directors' Report, 1901, George White papers, Bristol Archives.
3 The UK pre-decimal currency system divided the pound into 20 shillings (with symbol s) and each shilling into twelve pennies (d).
4 *Western Daily Press (WDP)*, 19 July 1901.
5 *Bristol Times and Mirror (BTM)*, 1 August 1901.

In 1907, an American report on 'Municipal and Private Utilities' compared the terms and conditions of privately owned tramways companies, including Bristol Tramways, with those of publicly owned systems in Glasgow, Liverpool, London and Manchester. Tramways employees in Bristol worked 70 hours per week compared to the average 57 hours in the municipal undertakings. They were also paid significantly less. Bristol tramways' drivers were paid £1/5s/6d (£1.27½) per week, compared to the average wage of £1/12s/8d (£1.63) on the municipal tramways. Fares on the private tramways were 65% higher than the municipal average.* Although these figures refer to pay and conditions in 1907, they show that things had not improved significantly since 1901 and, more importantly, that the Bristol Tramways Company demanded longer hours and paid lower wages than municipally owned tramways operations in other cities.

*National Civic Federation, Municipal and Private Operations of Public Utilities. (New York, 1907).

improvements in their working conditions. As Ben Tillett[6] stated in a speech at the Horsefair on 4th August 1901, "Mr White has given them a lesson in monopoly. This arch-monopolist of Bristol has told the men that they have no right, as free men, to enter into a combination to protect their interests because he says he is their master".[7]

Tillett's speech went on, "In sleepy old Bristol, they have given their streets away to a professional speculative capitalist".[8]

George White

The 'speculative capitalist' referred to by Tillett was George White, brother of Samuel and Chairman of the Tramways Company. From humble beginnings—he was born in Kingsdown to a painter and

6   Ben Tillett was the leader of the Dock, Wharf, Riverside and General Workers' Union. Born in Easton, Bristol in 1860, he left school at eight to work in a brickyard. He then had a succession of jobs before settling in the east end of London and working in the docks. In 1889 he emerged as the leader of the London dock strike, part of the wave of militant 'New Unionism' which swept the country.
7   *WDP*, 5 August 1901.
8   Ibid.

Sir George White, 1854-1916.

decorator father and a mother who had been a domestic servant—by 1901 he had become one of the most powerful businessmen in Bristol. His transition to wealthy businessman began when he secured a job in a local law firm as a junior clerk. Much of his work was concerned with company bankruptcies which gave him an insight into business finance. The law firm was also involved in advising investors on the establishment of the horse trams system in Bristol which gave him valuable experience, detailed knowledge and, crucially, business connections. He left the law firm and rose to become the Chairman and leading shareholder in the Tramways Company. He established a stockbroking firm and was, for many years, president of the Bristol Stock Exchange. He also became a leading shareholder in the Imperial Tramways Company, which operated services in Dublin, Middlesbrough and Reading, and in the London United Tramways Company which operated in west London. His extensive business interests included the Bristol-based Western Wagon and Property Company, dock companies in Bristol, Sharpness and South Wales, and railway companies in the Bristol area, in the South Wales valleys and in India; he owned shares and was closely involved in the affairs of the Taff Vale Railway company. White was a leading figure in the local Conservative Party and was highly ambitious and a shrewd and ruthless businessman.[9]

The national context

'New unions', which included the Dock, Wharf, Riverside and General Workers' Union and the National Union of Gas Workers and General Labourers, emerged in the late 1880s. After successful strikes on the London docks and at a gas works in East London, these unions expanded into other parts of the country and into other industries. They differed to the older, craft-based unions in that they recruited previously non-unionised unskilled and semi-skilled workers across a range of different industries. They were also more militant, being much more prepared to use the strike weapon.

In the years after the emergence of 'new unions', trade unions both locally and nationally came under severe pressure from an employers' counter-offensive. John Saville, writing in 1967, showed how "through all the decade of the 1890s and well into the new century, a hostility developed towards trade unionism in general and new unionism in

9 C. Harvey and J. Press, 'Sir George White of Bristol, 1854-1916', (Bristol Historical Association, 1989).

£50 REWARD.

THE HOUSE OF LORDS HAVING LAST WEEK DECIDED IN AN ACTION AGAINST A TRADES UNION THAT

WATCHING OR BESETTING

OR CAUSING TO BE WATCHED OR BESET ANY OF THE WORKS AND PREMISES OF THE COMPANY, OR THE APPROACHES THERETO, OR THE PLACES OF RESIDENCE, OR ANY PLACE WHERE THEY MAY HAPPEN TO BE, OF *ANY WORKMAN EMPLOYED* BY OR *PROPOSING TO WORK FOR* THE COMPANY, FOR THE *PURPOSE OF PERSUADING* OR OTHERWISE PREVENTING PERSONS *FROM WORKING FOR THE COMPANY* OR INDUCING ANY PERSONS WHO ARE WORKING FOR THE COMPANY TO COMMIT A BREACH OF THEIR ENGAGEMENTS

IS ILLEGAL,

THE BRISTOL TRAMWAYS AND CARRIAGE COMPANY, LIMITED, hereby give PUBLIC NOTICE that they will pay a REWARD of FIFTY POUNDS to any person or persons who shall give such INFORMATION as shall lead to the conviction of any person or persons for committing any of the before-mentioned offences against anyone in the employ or proposing to enter the employ of the Bristol Tramways Company.

For and on behalf of the Company,

SAMUEL WHITE,

Managing Director.

Offices of the Company, 31st July, 1901.

An advertisement placed in Bristol newspapers on and from 1st August 1901. It refers to the Taff Vale judgment and claims that this had outlawed peaceful picketing. In fact, picketing had already been ruled an offence by the judgment in Lyons v. Wilkins in 1896.

particular that bordered on the hysterical".[10] Employers across a range of industries combined to combat the unions. The Shipping Federation, founded in 1890, and the National Free Labour Association (NFLA) in 1893, were set up to provide substitute labour to break strikes. The Engineering Employers' Federation (1896) was committed to collective action to protect individual firms and preserve their power to manage their own affairs. In taking the fight to the unions, these employers' organisations used blacklisting of known union activists, lock-outs and strike breakers. There were lock-outs in the mining, boot and shoe and engineering industries in the 1890s.

The use of the police and the army to counter picketing and contain union demonstrations became much more widespread in the 1890s. In Bristol, in December 1892, a march by locked-out dockworkers and striking female confectionery workers, was attacked by police and mounted soldiers in the centre of the city. This became known as 'Black Friday'. During the miners' lock-out of 1893, troops were sent to Yorkshire and two miners were shot dead in Featherstone. In 1900 a strike by grain porters and deal runners on Bristol docks was defeated after the intervention of the NFLA.

As the economy weakened, unemployment grew and trade union membership declined. The unions were also under severe legal pressure. In 1890 an Employers' Parliamentary Council was founded to pursue legal actions against the right to picket and to challenge the legal protection for union funds. Their efforts began to bear fruit in 1896 when the Court of Appeal ruled, in the case of Lyons v Wilkins, that picketing to persuade a person not to work was a 'nuisance' in common law and could therefore be subject to criminal proceedings. Just days before the start of the Bristol Tramways dispute, on 22nd July, the House of Lords delivered their judgment in the case of the Taff Vale Railway Company v the Amalgamated Society of Railway Servants, in which they declared that trade unions could be held liable for financial losses caused by strike action. The Bristol Tramways Company was very quick to exploit this, taking out adverts in the local press to publicise the judgment, although their emphasis was very much on the issue of whether picketing during an industrial dispute was illegal.[11]

---

10   J. Saville, 'Trade unions and Free Labour: The background to the Taff Vale Decision', in Briggs and Saville ed., *Essays in Labour History*, 1967
11   *WDP*, 1 August 1901. The same advert appeared in the *BTM*, and both newspapers ran the advert for several days.

The Taff Vale Railway Connection

The Taff Vale Railway operated between Merthyr Tydfil and Cardiff in South Wales, serving the large Dowlais Iron works in Merthyr and the many coal mines in the Taff and Rhondda valleys. Its shares were traded on the Bristol Stock Exchange and George White became a large shareholder in the company in the 1880s. In 1891, with the company facing growing competition and its profits beginning to decline, George White engineered a shareholders' revolt at a Special General Meeting held at the Royal Hotel in Bristol. This resulted in the existing chairman, Thomas Inskip, a Bristol solicitor and businessman, being ousted and a new Board of Directors being appointed.* Their agenda was an aggressive programme of cost-cutting and the maximisation of profits. Although George White did not himself take a position on the new board, it was clear that he was the power behind the throne. The local secretary of the Amalgamated Society of Railway Servants (ASRS) in South Wales summed up the union view of this change in leadership. "The advent of the new Board," he stated, "with its mission of greed, must cause a revival of that unrest among the rank and file which it was fondly hoped the agreements entered into by Mr. Inskip last year had terminated".* His words proved to be prophetic. In 1900 the Taff Vale Railway was hit by a two-week strike by the ASRS for higher wages and union recognition. The union did not win concessions from the Company, which had brought in strike breakers supplied by the National Free Labour Association, yet the Company still sued the union for damages once the strike was over. The Taff Vale judgment followed in 1901, with the union being fined £23,000 plus £19,000 in costs. The right to strike had effectively been nullified by this judgment.

*George White papers, Bristol Archives.

The 1901 lock-out

The first shots in the Tramways Company's battle with the union were fired in February 1901, when thirty 'spare' drivers petitioned the traffic manager for more regular work. The company sacked three men whom it considered to be the ringleaders. This did not stop more employees from joining the union, whilst the company kept a very close eye on the situation. In an interview with the press in late July, Samuel White stated that, "we had private information some time ago that it had been arranged that the Gas Workers' agent should be sent down to Bristol to endeavour, as they called it, to capture the Bristol tramway men". "The whole plan of campaign', he went on, "was prepared. They were to go amongst the men, sow seeds of dissension, get as many men as possible to join the union quietly and then to utilise them as agents for the remainder of the staff". He concluded that, "but for the advent of the organising secretary of this union, none of those misguided men and boys would have dreamt of such an act of treachery against their employers".[12] The Tramways Company demanded loyalty and obedience from its employees—whom it referred to as 'servants'—and was not prepared to accept any 'interference' in the company's affairs by 'outside' influences such as the union.

The simmering tensions came to a head on 17th July when seven employees were dismissed for being members of the union. The union called a meeting of its members on 18th July at the Shepherds' Hall in Old Market. The Company's ticket inspectors were sent along to the meeting to collect the names of those attending, as a result of which ninety-three more employees were dismissed on 27th July. The following day 310 union members employed by the company handed in their notices. This was the beginning of a dispute—part lock-out and part strike—between the union and the Company which continued throughout August and into September. The Company's management was placed on a war footing, with a select group of three directors—George and Samuel White and Joseph Wethered—meeting daily. They also compiled a log-book, listing the names of those dismissed for joining the union with comments by the ticket inspectors. Conductor Wiltshire was dismissed on 19th July for persuading others to join the union. Driver Banks was sacked after spending several nights at Brislington depot "preaching to others re. the union" and conductor Abrahams had been heard to

---

12 Samuel White, 'A complete refutation of the mis-statements of the agitators', BT&CC press release, in George White papers, Bristol Archives.

NATIONAL UNION OF GAS WORKERS
AND GENERAL LABOURERS.
BRISTOL AND SOUTH WESTERN DISTRICT.

ORGANIZE ! ORGANIZE ! ORGANIZE !

NOTICE TO THE

EMPLOYEES of the BRISTOL TRAMWAY & CARRIAGE CO.

A SPECIAL

MASS MEETING

OF MOTOR MEN, CONDUCTORS, and all others working for
the above Company,

WILL BE HELD IN THE

SHEPHERD'S HALL, OLD MARKET STREET,

ON

SUNDAY NEXT, JULY 21,

When all the above Workmen are earnestly requested to attend.

Chair to be taken at 9 a.m. by **Councillor W. BASTER.**

ADDRESSES will be delivered by **Mr. H. BRABHAM** (District Secretary of above
Union), **Mr. W. WHITFIELD** (Miners' Agent), **Councillor W. POPE**
(Branch Secretary, A.S.C.J.), **Mr. W. GORMAN** (District Secretary,
Dockers' Union), **H. PICARD** (General Organizer of above Union),
and other Prominent Trades Unionists.

The GAS WORKERS & GENERAL LABOURERS' UNION is a National one,
and has 336 Branches in the United Kingdom, and a Membership of over
50,000. It is the strongest Union of its character in the country. A Branch
of the above Union has been opened, and if the Tramway Workers of
Bristol desire better conditions of labour they can only obtain
them by a more thorough organization amongst themselves.

Intending Members may join any Morning from 9.30 till 11 a.m. or any Evening
except Wednesday from 6.30 till 8 p.m., at DISTRICT OFFICE, NEW STREET
BRITISH WORKMAN, ST. JUDE'S.

H. BRABHAM, *District Secretary.*

The opening double page spread in the company's logbook of the 1901 lock-
out. It shows very clearly how the company viewed the issues at stake in the
dispute. More pages are shown in the appendix.

Trades Union
AGITATION

Thursday 18 July 1901

Socialists organise
a
Meeting for Tramway Employees
at
Shepherds Hall
Old Mens Sct
21 July 1901

About 200 Drivers & Conductors
Attend Meeting.

On Monday 15 July Drivers J. Chivers and J. Merrett tried to persuade Con. F. Ricketts, in Victoria St on a car, to join the union. They said: "If a member of the union would get better pay and less hours and if any member got discharged through belonging to the union they would be compensated, &c." Had much to say.

G.C.

tell the gas workers, "we have got a union at last"; "bad conductor" was the inspector's judgment on him. Driver Gulliford of Brislington had been "agitating others to join the union" and talked of an eight-hour day. Conductor James of Hotwells was described as "useless, his inattention indicated union influence".[13]

In contrast to the belligerent tone of the Tramways Company's management, the leader of the Gas Workers' union in Bristol, Harold Brabham, did his best to lower the temperature. At a mass meeting on Broad Quay on 25th July, the *Western Daily Press* reported the "feeling was running high" and that there was a "strong inclination on the part of the men not to come to work on the following morning". Brabham advised them to keep working in order to show the company that "all they claimed was the right to join a union". He asked his members to show a "pacific bearing" as he made repeated requests to the company to accept arbitration, all of which were ignored.[14] His defensive attitude reflected the weak position that the union was in. Union membership among tramways employees covered little more than a third of the workforce so that, from the very start of the dispute, the company were able to maintain a basic service.

Support for the cause

Despite these difficulties, the spirits of the union members were high at the start of the dispute, buoyed by the widespread public support for their cause. A mass meeting at the Horsefair on Sunday 29th July attracted a crowd of three thousand.[15] Meetings and marches were held daily; lunchtime meetings were organised by the union and evening meetings by the Bristol Trades Council. There were also more spontaneous gatherings at important points in the tramways system—St Augustine's Bridge, Old Market Street, Brislington depot and outside the depots in Horfield and Bedminster. At one meeting in Old Market Street on 2nd August a reporter from the *Bristol Times and Mirror* estimated that the crowd numbered around five thousand. The August Bank Holiday weekend saw a well-attended mass meeting in the Horsefair on Sunday 4th August at which the Dockers' Union leader, Ben Tillett, was the main speaker. The momentum was maintained through the following week. An evening meeting at Brislington depot on Tuesday 6th August was

13   George White papers, Bristol Archives.
14   *WDP*, 26 July 1901.
15   *BTM*, 1 August 1901.

Brislington tramway depot drawn by Samuel Loxton.

attended by an estimated one thousand people. On Sunday 11th August there was a large attendance at a march through the city, followed by a mass meeting on the Downs.

The support of the Trades Council was important in rallying the wider labour movement to get behind the tramwaymen. Collections were held at public meetings and union branches, such as the Bristol Miners' Association, made donations. By 19th August it was reported that £500 had been raised. This was distributed as strike pay at a rate of ten shillings per week. Trade union branches from a wide range of industries passed resolutions in support. These included the Bristol Miners' Association, the National Union of Boot and Shoe Operatives, the Amalgamated Society of Carpenters and Joiners, the National Shop Assistants' Union, the Typographical Association and the Plasterers Union. Support came also from non-union organisations. Several bible classes associated with non-conformist chapels, such as the Bethel Free Methodist chapel and the Castle Men's Bible Class, together with the Retail Fruiterers and Greengrocers' Association and the Bristol and District Building Industries Federation, expressed their moral support.[16]

16 *WDP*, 7 August, 8 August, 15 August 1901.

BRISTOL TRAMWAYS & CARRIAGE COMPANY, Limited.

(BY TELEGRAM.)

ANOTHER IMPORTANT DECISION BY THE HOUSE OF LORDS.

It will be remembered that the House of Lords a week or two ago decided a VERY IMPORTANT CASE AGAINST PICKETING by TRADES UNIONISTS in connection with the TAFF VALE RAILWAY.

YESTERDAY, MONDAY, AUGUST 5TH, the House of Lords gave another important decision. In this new case the Belfast Journeymen Butchers' Society had, in order to compel the employer to dispense with the non-Union men, brought pressure to bear on his customers to cease dealing with the master butcher until he should dismiss the non-Union assistants, and they also brought pressure to bear on the master himself by threatenings. The employer had sued the Union for damages, which the Courts had awarded. The Society, however, carried an appeal against judgment to the House of Lords.

THE HOUSE OF LORDS on Monday dismissed the Trade Society's appeal and DETERMINED THAT THE ACTS OF THE SOCIETY and its members were wrongful and malicious, and THAT THE TRADES UNION SOCIETY AND ITS FUNDS WERE RESPONSIBLE FOR ALL DAMAGES AWARDED.

NOTICE is Hereby Given that THE FUNDS OF ANY TRADES UNION SOCIETIES, whose official leaders have taken part in Bristol in the attack upon the Tramways Company, and who have been suggesting to the public the means by which the Company shall be made to lose traffic, WILL BE HELD ANSWERABLE FOR ALL LOSS AND DAMAGES which may be INCURRED by the BRISTOL TRAMWAYS AND CARRIAGE COMPANY, LTD., in consequence of such malicious and illegal action.

SAMUEL WHITE, Managing Director.

Offices of the Company, 6th August, 1901.

An advertisement which was placed in the local press from 7th August. It refers to both the Taff Vale judgment and the judgment against boycotting in the case of Quinn v. Leatham.

The Company's response

At the beginning of the dispute tram services were severely curtailed during the daytime and no trams at all were run after 8pm. The Company, however, took immediate steps to get more trams running. On 1st August, a tented camp was set up at Brislington depot, equipped to provide food, drink and lodging for strikebreakers, and on 3rd August the first of many men supplied by the National Free Labour Association arrived in Bristol. The Company records do not reveal how many strikebreakers were brought in, but press reports talked of men being brought in from Lancashire and Cheshire, from Leeds and from Reading.[17] In his autobiography, William Collison the founder of the NFLA,[18] devoted a whole chapter to his part in the events of August 1901. He wrote about receiving a visit from James Clifton Robinson, a close friend of George White, who asked him to supply strikebreakers, whatever the cost to the Tramways Company.

The first group of strikebreakers were taken by train from Paddington on Saturday 3rd August. Collison recounted how he "received information that thousands of miners were waiting at Bristol [Temple Meads station] to give us a greeting, so I determined to outwit them".[19] They left the train at Bath and took a local stopping train to St. Anne's Park near Brislington, from where they were transported in brakes to the Brislington depot. More strikebreakers arrived in the coming days. "One of my great difficulties", wrote Collison, "was to keep the pickets from encroaching too near to the depot, so I had it surrounded with barbed wire entanglements, charged with electricity; then I had a revolving searchlight posted".[20] He concluded, disingenuously, that, "looking back at the Bristol strike I can unhesitatingly say that it stands out as a plain and straightforward fight to a finish between employer and employed, with no outside interference of any description".[21]

Despite twenty-seven men from Reading returning home after they learned "the true facts about the dispute",[22] the Company was able to steadily increase the tram service during the first week of August. The night service was resumed on 12th August. On 14th August it was

---

17   *WDP*, 9 August 1901.
18   William Collison, *The Apostle of Free Labour*, 1913.
19   *Ibid*.
20   *Ibid*.
21   *Ibid*.
22   *WDP*, 6 August 1901.

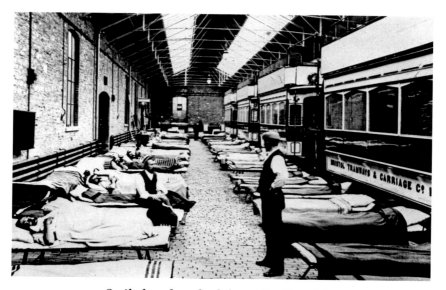

Strikebreakers bed down for the night.

reported that the Company had filled all vacancies for drivers.[23] The camp at Brislington was closed the following day and the National Free Labour Association strikebreakers were withdrawn. As far as the Company was concerned the dispute was now over and the battle had been won.

This was not yet the union's assessment of the situation. Daily lunchtime meetings continued. On 19th August between four and five hundred people attended a meeting at Broad Quay. The following weekend, on Sunday 25th August, there was a well-attended march to the zoo.[24] Gradually, however, the crowds diminished. Once a week the union distributed strike pay to its members at the mid-day meeting. On Saturday 31st August, for example, 356 men were paid—fewer than the original 430 men involved in the dispute, but not a sign of a total collapse in support. Lunchtime meetings continued for another two weeks but the last recorded meeting was on Thursday 12th September. Bristol Tramways and Carriage Company remained a non-union employer. In December the Company celebrated its victory with a slap-up meal and musical entertainment for its 'loyal' employees at the Colston Hall. To reward their loyalty, and to mark what George White called a "personal

23   *WDP*, 14 August 1901.
24   *WDP*, 26 August 1901.

bond of sympathy" between the Company and its loyal employees, silver medals were given to those who had continued working during the dispute.[25]

More legal action

It is clear that strike action alone, when little more than a third of the workforce was involved, had limited chances of success against a Company which was prepared to use every means at its disposal to defeat the union. There was, however, a possible additional weapon in the union's arsenal. From the early days of the dispute there was talk about, and enthusiasm for, a public boycott of the trams. On 31st July, at a crowded evening meeting in Old Market Street, there were calls for a public boycott.[26] On 2nd August, according to the *Bristol Times and Mirror*, "several gangs of factory hands notified the union that they were boycotting the trams", although which factories were involved was not made clear. On 7th August the union appealed to the public for a boycott. A meeting at St George's Park gates on 7th August passed a resolution in favour of a boycott.

The law, however, was very much on the Company's side. On 5th August, the Law Lords delivered their judgment in the case of Quinn v Leathem, declaring that an attempt by a trade union, the Belfast Journeymen Butchers' and Assistants' Association, to organise a customer boycott of Leathem's butchers, with which the union was in dispute, was a 'conspiracy to injure' and that the company could sue the union for damages. In response, the Bristol Tramways Company instructed solicitors, on 7th August, to issue writs against the Gas Workers' union, an action which was taken "in view of the House of Lords' decision on Monday".[27] Despite strong public support for a boycott, and the many individual and group decisions to stop riding on the trams, the union was constrained from organising a concerted campaign to boycott the trams.

At the beginning of the dispute the crowds which gathered in places such as Old Market and Brislington depot were noisy but relatively peaceful. There was, however, growing frustration and anger at the Company's use of strike breakers to keep trams running, which resulted in verbal and physical assaults on tram drivers and attempts to stop the

25 George White papers, Bristol Archives.
26 *WDP*, 1 August 1901.
27 *WDP*, 8 August 1901.

trams from running. This prompted the Company to place adverts in the local press offering rewards for information in order to prosecute the perpetrators. Prosecutions in the Police Court were paid for by the Company. On 1st August, for example, James Chandler, aged nineteen, was charged with throwing stones at driver Joseph Neath in Old Market.[28] On 3rd August a man was sent for trial at the Quarter Sessions on a charge of placing rubber on the tram tracks. On 16th August, tramcars were physically stopped by crowds in St. Phillips, Lawrence Hill and St. George. On 26th August a large crowd in Colston Avenue stopped a tram by disconnecting its overhead arms.[29] In all, between 2nd August and 20th September, the Company brought 47 prosecutions to the Police Court. Most of the accused were found guilty, with a typical sentence being a fine of ten shillings plus costs, or fourteen days in prison. Some were immediately committed to prison, with sentences ranging from two to three weeks, sometimes with hard labour. So many cases were brought before the courts that special sessions had to be arranged, and the magistrates pleaded with the Company, on 15th August, that "as this dispute appears to be at an end, they thought the Company should consider whether it was advisable to proceed with other cases of assault".[30] This appeal fell on deaf ears as there were more prosecutions after this date than before.

Later developments

The cab drivers in the employ of the Bristol Tramways and Carriage Company were the next group of workers to try to get union representation. In November 1911, thirty men were dismissed for attending a Trades Council meeting. Two hundred of their fellow cab drivers then went on strike in support.[31] As with the tramways dispute in 1901, the cab drivers were defeated by a company which was resolutely opposed to allowing any 'outside interference' in its business. After the outbreak of war in 1914, however, the industrial relations landscape changed to favour the unions. Firstly, the pressures of wartime inflation and the intensification of labour led to a growth in trade union membership across the board. Secondly, in a bid to maintain continuity of production and avoid strikes, the government and trade unions concluded the

---

28   *BTM*, 2 August 1901.
29   *WDP*, 27 August 1901.
30   *WDP*, 16 August 1901.
31   *Evening Mail*, 13 November 1911.

BRISTOL TRAMWAYS & CARRIAGE COMPANY, Limited.

WHEREAS there is evidently an organised conspiracy on the part of certain dastardly scoundrels to injure the Company, *utterly regardless of the lives and safety of the public of Bristol*, and in order to encompass their vile purpose, they have maliciously designed and are still perpetrating a plan of placing obstructions, such as

IRON BOLTS & RIVETS, PIECES OF ROD IRON, STONES, &c.,

on the rails of the Tramways. The following offences having already been reported—

DATE.	PLACE.	OFFENCE.
Tuesday Night, 13th August.	Victoria Street (Opposite No. 129).	An Iron Bolt placed in rail.
Wednesday Night, 14th August.	Deanery Road (Opposite Norman Gateway).	An Iron Bolt and Rivet placed in one rail and a Length of Rod Iron in the other rail.
Wednesday Night, 14th August.	Kensington Hill, Brislington.	Eight Pieces of Rod Iron placed in rail.
Thursday Night, 15th August.	Bath Road (Opposite Kitchener's Terraces).	Iron Bolt placed in rail.
Thursday Night, 15th August.	Bath Road (Opposite Arno's Vale Convent).	Stones placed on rail.
Friday Mid-day, 16th August.	Near Bath Bridge.	Iron Bolt placed in rail.

NOW, THEREFORE, WE, the Bristol Tramways and Carriage Company, Limited, do hereby invite all law-abiding citizens to co-operate with us in the discovery of offenders, and we hereby give public notice that we will pay a

REWARD OF £100

to any person or persons who shall give such information as leads to the conviction and imprisonment of the persons guilty of the above-mentioned offences or of any similar outrage which may be committed after the publication of this notice.

For and on behalf of
THE BRISTOL TRAMWAYS & CARRIAGE CO., Ltd.,
SAMUEL WHITE, Managing Director.

Offices of the Company, 16th August, 1901.

An advert which appeared in the local press after 16th August, referring to numerous attempts to sabotage the tram lines and the company's determination to punish those responsible. There are no records to show how successful this appeal was but many people were prosecuted by the company.

The London United Tramways strike, 1909

George White's determination to keep the trade unions out of his business was not confined to the Bristol Tramways Company. In 1909 there was a strike on the London United Tramways (LUT), part of White's Imperial Tramways group, which operated services in west London. This followed a very similar pattern to the Bristol Tramways dispute of 1901, unsurprisingly since the Managing Director of LUT was Sir James Clifton Robinson who was a tramways engineer and close friend of George White. So closely did they work together that George White kept a folder of press cuttings and other documents relating to the LUT strike. The dispute began with dismissals of employees who had joined the Amalgamated Association of Tramways and Vehicle Workers, which led to a strike by the remaining trade union members at the company. As in Bristol, the company prosecuted many strikers and their supporters in the Police Court and also used strike breakers supplied by the National Free Labour Association. Within a few days the strike had been defeated to the delight of White, Robinson, and the NFLA. In a letter to Robinson on 13th April, a spokesperson for the NFLA said, "We note you have successfully dealt with the malcontents in your employ, and that the so-called strike did not interfere with your service during the holiday". The letter went on to claim that "We could have placed at your disposal 1,500 competent motor drivers within twelve hours of receiving your instructions".*

* George White papers, Bristol Archives.

Treasury Agreement of 1915 which imposed compulsory arbitration on employers and unions in any disputes.

In 1917, the London and Provincial Licensed Vehicle Workers' Union began recruiting among Bristol Tramways employees, including the women who, since 1916, had been employed as conductors to release men for war service. True to form, the Bristol Tramways Company refused to recognise the union or to accede to its demand for a wage increase and shorter hours for the women. In October 1917, a strike followed. When other unions in the city declared that they were considering sympathy strike action, the Ministry of Labour intervened and the strike ended.[32] The union was finally recognised by the company but only on the basis that union members could be part of a Works' Committee structure that the company established for resolving disputes. This was an uneasy compromise and one which brought only temporary peace. There were two short-lived strikes in 1918; the first, in April, involved drivers on the Bedminster and Ashton Vale line, who objected to having to work with non-union labour, and a second strike in August when union members stopped work in pursuit of a demand for women who "were doing men's work" to receive equal pay.

As some 2,280 male tramways employees had either volunteered or been conscripted into the armed forces, the company had employed women as conductors since 1917. When men were demobilised in 1919, they expected to return to their jobs on the tramways but, by mid-1919 only 650 had been re-employed. Discontent among the thousands of unemployed ex-servicemen came to a head in April 1920 when there were daily demonstrations across the city. Trams were attacked and women conductors were abused. The company gave in to the pressure and dismissed the women, giving each of them £5 in compensation.

By the early 1920s, with the onset of the severe post-war depression, the gains made by tramwaymen in their wages and conditions as a result of union membership came under renewed attack by the company, in common with tramways and bus workers across the country. Wages were cut and hours increased.

The continuing tensions between company and union came to a head in 1923 when a lightning strike by union members began on the evening of 4th June. Although the immediate cause of the strike was a wage dispute, the underlying cause was the company's refusal to negotiate with the trade union committee, insisting instead that it would only deal with its own works' committee. In other words, trade union recognition, and all that that involved, had been withdrawn. The company warned that strikers would be dismissed and began employing strike breakers. In a letter to the National Secretary of the Transport and General Workers' Union (TGWU),[33] William Verdon Smith, the Managing Director of the company refused to engage in any negotiations with the union. "The members of your union in our employment", he wrote, "have ceased work without notice on several occasions during recent years. This is a

32 WDP, 25 October 1917, and following dates.
33 The London and Provincial Licensed Vehicle Workers' Union had been absorbed into the TGWU in 1921.

Registered under the Trade Union Acts, No. 945.   Established 1894.   'Phone: 7189 GERRARD.

1 aug 1917

LONDON AND PROVINCIAL UNION
OF
LICENSED VEHICLE WORKERS.
(Formerly London Cabdrivers' Trade Union.)
Chief Office: 30, GERRARD STREET, W. 1.

Affiliated to the Parliamentary Committee of the Trades Union Congress, the Labour Party, the General Federation of Trade Unions, the Triple Combine (i.e., Miners, Railwaymen, and Transport Workers), London Trades Council, and Local Trades and Labour Councils.

Copyright.

IMPORTANT

TO ALL VEHICLE WORKERS.

A Plain Talk with the Non-Unionist.

Will you let us have your attention for a few moments, and we will give you a few reasons why you should become a **TRADE UNIONIST?**

You are a **WAGE-WORKER**, and the commodity you have to sell is your labour. You want to get the best price you can for that; you want a good wage—the very best wage you can get. You want good conditions as well.

Wages have not risen to keep pace with the enormous rise in the price of the necessaries of life. It is up to **YOU** to help us to raise the status of all Vehicle Workers.

CONTRIBUTIONS.

Cab and 'Bus Drivers	6d. per week.
Private Chauffeurs	6d. ,,
Tram Drivers and Conductors	4d. ,,
Motor Commercial and Lorry Drivers ...	4d. ,,
Motor Contract and Cartage Drivers... ...	4d. ,,
Garage Hands and Loaders	3d. ,,
Juveniles up to 18 years	2d. ,,

BENEFITS.

Death (Member and Member's Wife).
Accident Pay.
Strike Pay.
Lock-Out Pay.
Victimisation Pay.
Legal Assistance to any extent for matters arising out of employment.

JOIN UP ! You have nothing to lose and everything to gain.

A recruiting leaflet from the London and Provincial Union of Licensed Vehicle Workers issued in August 1917.

Tram on the Bedminster and Ashton Vale line.

state of things which the company cannot tolerate and therefore we must proceed to obtain the services of a body of men who have more sense of responsibility for the carrying out of their duties. With that object, the company are now engaging new employees and are not prepared to take part in a discussion, either formal or informal".[34] By 8th June, two hundred tramways employees had been dismissed, the union had been defeated and the Bristol Tramways and Carriage Company was once again a non-union employer. During the general strike of 1926, Bristol trams and buses continued to operate.

"A union at last"

By the 1930s there had been significant changes to the management and ownership of the Tramways Company. Samuel White died in 1928 and was succeeded as chairman by William Verdon Smith, a nephew of George White. In 1929, the Great Western Railway bought a large share in the company and, by the mid-1930s it was jointly owned by the GWR and Thomas Tilling. Verdon Smith stood down in 1935, ending the long association between the White family and the Bristol Tramways. During these years, the TGWU was steadily recruiting tramways (and

34 George White papers, Bristol Archives.

Distributed Fri. 24.8.17

Telephone: 7180 GERRARD.

Registered under the Trades Union Acts, No. 945

ESTAB 1894

London and Provincial Union of Licensed Vehicle Workers.

(Formerly LONDON CABDRIVERS' TRADE UNION.)

CHIEF OFFICE : **39, GERRARD STREET, W. I.**

Affiliated to the Parliamentary Committee of the Trades Union Congress, the Labour Party, the General Federation of Trade Unions, the Triple Combine (i.e., Miners, Railwaymen, and Transport Workers), London Trades Council, and Local Trades and Labour Councils.

TO THE VEHICLE WORKERS OF BRISTOL.

May we claim your attention for a few moments?

A MEETING

WILL BE HELD AT THE

PEOPLE'S PICTURE PALACE,

BALDWIN STREET, BRISTOL,

On SUNDAY, AUGUST 26th, 1917,

AT 10.30 A.M.

Chairman : T. C. LEWIS

(Secretary Bristol Trades and Labour Council).

Speakers :

Mr. ERNEST BEVIN

(National Organiser Dockers' Union),

Councillor G. W. BROWN

(Organiser National Union of Railwaymen),

Mr. V. DESPRES

(Organising Secretary Ships' Stewards' Union),

GEO. SANDERS

(Organiser Licensed Vehicle Workers' Union),

See Bristol Tramways at Back [P.T.O.]

Handbill for a rally of tramway workers. The handwritten note was penned by a company representative.

TRANSPORT & GENERAL WORKERS' UNION.

BRISTOL DISTRICT. :: Area Office: Tailors Court, Bristol,

TRAMWAY DISPUTE.

Fellow Workers,

We are holding a **Special Meeting** at the **Kingsley Hall, Old Market,** on **Sunday Morning** at **10.30 a.m.,** and we make an earnest appeal to you to attend.

We are aware a large number of you have expressed that you were misled by some of the statements circulated, which induced you to return to work. It is therefore necessary that you should know the truth officially from the Union and its members. Probably counter efforts will be made to prevent your attending. We therefore appeal to everyone to **Assert Your Manhood** and not leave your Mates stranded.

(*Signed*) JAMES GARMSTON,
Area Secretary.

Transport and General Workers Union leaflet from the 1923 strike.

bus) employees and opened negotiations with the company on union recognition and a procedural agreement.

In 1936 the City Corporation once again had the option to purchase the tramways, an option which had been rejected on every previous occasion. The Labour Party had since before 1914 advocated the municipal ownership of the tramways and, with a large and growing number of councillors, was on the brink of taking control of the council (which it finally did in 1937).

Tilling and the TGWU, each for their own reasons, saw the opportunity for a compromise deal. In 1936, the company recognised the union, signed a procedural agreement and promised no compulsory redundancies if, as the company proposed, the tram services were closed

The Bristol Tramways & Carriage Company, Ltd.

NOTICE TO STAFF

The majority of the Late Duty Staff last night ran their Cars to Depot before scheduled times in utter disregard of all discipline and the convenience of the public, and others have absented themselves from duty to-day. The Management were given no warning or notice of any intention to cease work and certain Members of the Transport and General Workers' Union took upon themselves to order cessation of work.

ALL EMPLOYEES ARE HEREBY WARNED THAT MEN FAILING TO REPORT FOR DUTY AT THE CORRECT TIME ON WEDNESDAY, THE 6TH INSTANT, WILL BE DEEMED TO HAVE LEFT THE SERVICE OF THE COMPANY, AND MUST RETURN THEIR UNIFORM TO THEIR RESPECTIVE DEPOTS BY SATURDAY, THE 9TH INSTANT.

The Company give good wages and conditions to their employees and expect loyal service in return and an uninterrupted performance of duty in the interest of the public.

SYDNEY E. SMITH,
Manager.

Tramways Centre,
5th June, 1923.

EDWARD EVERARD, PRINTER, BRISTOL.

Tramways Company 'Notice to Staff' from the 1923 strike.

and replaced by buses. As far as ownership and control of the tram and bus services was concerned, the company would accept a partnership with the City Corporation. The TGWU, with its considerable influence within the local Labour Party and the wider labour movement, threw its weight behind Tilling's scheme and this was approved by the City Council, despite significant opposition from the Labour left.[35]

Conclusion

The recognition of the TGWU by the Bristol Tramways Company was the culmination of thirty-five years of struggle. Despite facing personal hardship and threats of prosecution, the majority of the tramway employees who went on strike in 1901 did not give up on their belief that they would only be able to improve their pay and conditions with union support. On that occasion, the company won the battle but the desire, and need, for union representation was not eradicated. The cabmen tried to secure union rights in 1911, only to suffer the same fate as the tramwaymen in 1901. Union recognition of a kind was grudgingly conceded in 1917, only to be snatched away again in 1923. When union rights were finally conceded in 1936, there was no triumphalism on the part of the union—in contrast to the company's Loyalty Night in 1901. The Company did not suffer as a consequence of allowing an 'outside body' to represent its workers. In the short term it gained union support for its continuing involvement in public transport in Bristol and, it is arguable, in the longer term, there were many benefits for it in establishing a procedural agreement to regulate conflict within the workplace.

---

35   *WDP*, 25 May 1937.

Appendix

No	Name	Statement
1	Driver J. Merrett, riding about on cars forth pass
2	Conductor J. Chivers	Do
3	Driver " Flook	Do
4	Driver " Cockram Fitland Rd & Elsewhere who
5	Conductor Wiltshire. Persudding Conductor &
6	On Saturday 13 July. Driver Ayres driving recklessly
7	Driver Smart Absent himself from duty Sunday
8	Con. Reece, S.Hill. Insolence to Inman Insubodmation &.
9	Driver O. Martin, not take his car at Centre Sat. afternd
10	Driver Banks off duty 7 30 pm Bus. At Brislington sever
11	Driver Warren Hotwells. Busy early part of last week .
12	Driver Warren Knowle told Taylor Tuesday 21 July
13	Con. Pratten Hotwells. Abrahams heard him tell Gasworkers
14	Driver R. Whittington curses Driver S. Richards who ref
15	Driver Heathcoate shouting at Wells Rd Junction Friday
16	Sunday 21 July Driver C. Day abused Henry Martin at
17	Bitton. Dr J. Hopkins accused of Stone being at Meeting. Stone
18	Driver Shugar S.H. joined Union Sunday 21 VII.
19	Driver White S.H. Do	Do	Just
20	Driver Hayes S.H. Do	Do	Just
21	Driver H. Davies S.A.	Do	Persudding
22	Driver B.B. Thomas Kwood	Do	(?)
23	Driver F. Williams Kwood	Do	Gast. Red.
24	Driver G. Bridgland (Late Con.) Do Gast. Red.
25	Driver W.E.H. Bright. W.Ha.	Do	Is a member
26	Driver C. Church W.Ha	Do	Is a member
27	Driver Glastonbury S.H.	Do
27	Driver Piper W.Rd	an Old Unionist before
28	Driver Hutton W.Rd	Joined Union Sun. 21 VII
29	Driver Elliott S.H.	Do
30	Condr Bencher W.Rd	Do

The Bristol Tramways and Carriage Company logbook of the 1901 lock-out.

No	Name	Statement
31	Con. Bowden W.Rd	Joined union Sun. 21. VII
32	Con. Cook W.Rd	Do
33	Con. Green W.Rd	Do
34	Con. Ball W.Rd	Do
35	Con. & Goldsworthy W.Rd	Do
36	Driver Widgery (spare Hor.)	Do ✓
37	Driver A Vicary (do)	Do ✓
38	Driver H. Tiley (Spare Bed.)	Do
39	Driver W. Rapps (do)	Do
40	Con. Vincent. Hor. Been sick. Declared off funds on
41	Driver J Watkins (S. Hill) says to have originated plan
42	Driver Forward (S Hill)	Do
43	Driver Riggs (W.Rd.) told Branne they had joined
44	Driver J. Clements (East. Red) Seen by Parish leaving the place
45	Driver Simpson ('Ea owle)	do
46	" E. Cole (do)	do
47	" Ayliffe (Henham)	do
48	" G. Williams (do)	do
49	" Nicholls (do)	do
50	" J Tudor (do)	do
51	" J. Sweet (E wood)	do
52	" R. Richards (do)	do
53	Cond. E Hitchins (East. Red) ✓	do
54	" J. Malpas (do) ✓	do
55	" J. Willis (do) ✓	do
56	" H. Goldsworthy (Conda. Red) ✓	do
57	" J Tudor (Henham)	do
58	" H. Broom (Red) Told Con. Farr. that he had joined
59	" F. Sinkiss (")	Do
60	" J. Lange (")	Do

Remarks

	✱ ✓ D⁰ 27 VII ½ Weeks Wages
	D⁰ 25. 7. 01. Paid week to wages
	✓ D⁰ 27 VII ½ Weeks Wages
Attended meeting outside Depot	See no. 103.
Bad Con?.. Persuade others.	✓ D⁰ T. 23 VII Paid Weeks Wages
	✓ D⁰ 27 VII Paid Weeks Wage
	✓ D⁰ 27 VII Paid Weeks wages
	J. 1 T. 23 VII. Paid Weeks Wages
	D⁰ T. 23 VII Paid Weeks wages
Mon 22. In streets with discharged men	D⁰ 24 VII Paid Weeks wages.
of hiring Breaks to run to Meeting. ✓	D⁰ 27 VII Paid Weeks Wages
Do	O
union	✓ D⁰ 27 VII Paid Weeks Wages
Hall Sunday 21. 7. 01. Another (A.E.) Saw him there.	✓ D⁰ 27 VII ½ W. Wages
do	✓ D⁰ 23. VII. Paid Weeks wages.
do	Has not joined. E.C.
do	See No. 75.
do	D⁰ 26 VII Paid weeks wages
do	D⁰ 26 VII Paid Weeks wages
do	No driver "Endor" Wardismured
do	✓ D⁰ 27 VII ½ Weeks Wages
do	✓ D⁰ 27 VII ½ Weeks wages
do	D⁰ 25. 7.01 Paid weeks wages
do	D⁰ 25. 7. 01. Paid weeks wages
do	D⁰ 25. 7. 01. Paid weeks wages.
do	See No. 35.
do	D⁰ 26 VII Paid Weeks wages
union. Urged him to do so. Refused	D⁰ 24. VII Paid Weeks wages
Do	D⁰ 24. VII. Paid Weeks Wages
DO	✓ D⁰ 24. VII Paid Weeks Wages

No.	Name	Line	State
61	Cond. Coolke.	S. H. ✓	Told Ashcroft.
62	" Boucher.	"	
63	" J Cook.	" ✓	This Con. wants to
64	Driver Sheppard.	"	Reposted by
65	" Neel	"	(late Cond.)
66	Con Green	"	
67	" G. Bentley	D. Rd ✓	
68	" G. Bentley	S. H.	
69	" R. Creech	D. Rd ✓	
70	" Neale.	"	
71	" H. Irwin.	"	
72	" Clark.	S. H.	
73	" Cole.	"	
72	Driver A Cook	Brd ?	Distributed several leaflets
73	" Gallop	Horfd	Depreciate Company
74	" Had	Kingswood	Asked Driver Thomas
75	" Ayliff	Hanham	Attended Meeting
76	" Gappard	S. H.	Do
77	" H Coles	Bushy Park	Told Wringer 23rd he had joined
78	" W. Woodbury	Red. Fork.	Told Hyett 22 July he had
79	" R. Williams	Horfield	
80	Condtr G. Peacock	Bedmstr	
81	" G. Blaby	"	
82	Driver Gullyford	Brislington	Three months before
83	Condtr Smith	Staple Hill	Attended Meeting outside
84	" Harris	"	do.
85	" Willcox	"	do.
86	" Curtis	"	do
87	" Westcott	"	do.
88	Driver F Goodwin	Horfd	Night of Meeting Goodwin foll'd Do
89	Driver W Foxe	Red.	Threatens to fight another
90	Con. M. Cook	Hotwells	Joined Union
91	Con. G. James	Do	Useless. His in-

ment.	Remark.
Jones 21.7.01 [23rd Adjourned Union adourned Meeting 22nd]	D° 25.7.01. Paid weeks wages
	✓ D° 27 VII Pd Weeks wages
fined W. Harrison for not joining	D° 25.7.01. Paid weeks wages
Ricketts joined 22.7.01	✓ D° 27 VII Pd Weeks wages
do.	✓ D° 27 VII Pd Weeks Wage
do.	See No. 33
do.	D° 25.7.01 Paid weeks wages
do.	✓ D° 27 VII Pd Weeks wages
do.	D° 25.7.01 Paid weeks wages
do. Attended Meeting outside depot SH 22nd	✓ D° 27 VII Pd Weeks Wages
do (persuaded by Dr. Church)	✓ D° 27 VII Pd Weeks wages
do.	D° 26 VII Paid Weeks wages
do. Attended meeting 22nd again	✓ D° 27 VII Pd Weeks Wages
Talked freely of Union. Grumbler.	✓ D° 24 July 01. Paid Weeks Wages
+ Insolent Manner. Visit Union A.m. to join	D° 25.7.01. Paid weeks wages
to Join 23rd. Thomas told Castle	D° 24 July 01. Paid Weeks Wages.
Sunday 22nd	✓ D° 24 July 01. Paid Week's Wages.
Monday outside Staple Hill Dy WR. Drunken	D° 24. VII. Paid Weeks Wages
Said probably would Striken a day or two.	D° 25.7.01. Paid Weeks Wages.
Joined Union. No interest says he except to stand up for men's rights	✓ D° 27 VII Pd Weeks Wages
	D° 25.7.01. Paid weeks wages.
	D° 25.7.01. Paid weeks wages.
	D° 25.7.01. Paid weeks wages
was agitating Other to join Union. Talks of 8 hours a day.	D° 25.7.01. Paid weeks Wages
Depot.	
Atwell of Gibbs. cursed them, call "blacklegs" for not attending	D° 25.7.01. Paid weeks wage.
Driver who refuses to join Union.	D° 25.7.01. Paid weeks wage.
	D° 25.7.01. Paid weeks wages
Attention indicates union influence	✓ D° 25.7.01 Paid weeks wage.

No	Name		
92	Car Washers Jones	Brislington	Joined Union
93	" Bees	Do	A member
94	McDowell, Strongs N. Staff	Do	A member
95	S. Durban Do	Do	A member
96	J Barrett Do Day Staff	Do	A member
97	Dr. Reynolds.	S.H. (?)	Advocated
98	" Pick.	Bed. (?)	Tellis props at Nork or sent to the office
99	Dr Merriott	SH	Advocated
100	Dr W. Stokes	Horfield	Under Union Influence
101	Dr G Shepherd	Staff. Hill	W. Taylor heard him tell
102	Dr G King	Do	Unwrust
103	Con. Ball	Do	Do
104	Con. A Martin	W.& Rd Sme	At Redland 25 VII Shouted
105	Con. F. Knight	Redland Green Sme	Has told Insp. W Brown
106	Con. N. Welsh	Hotwells	Joined Union
107	Con. W. Wood	"	Do
108	Con. E. Wood	"	Do
109	Con Lomase	"	Do a√
110	Con. Ford	Knowle	Do
111	Con. Probert	East. Red	Do
112	Con. Powell .	Horfd	Con. Ricketts
113	Con Hendy	Do	Do
114	Con. F. Heisler	Do	Do
115	Con. Worthington	Do	Do
116	Driver Malcolm	Knowle	Attended Meeting
117	" Kale	Busby Park	Do (with Horfield)
118	" New Combe	East. Red	Do
119	' Richards	Knowle	Do
120	Con. F. Seaman	East. Red	Do
121	" Cox	Knowle	Do
122	" Henley	Brislington	Do
123	" J. Wall	Horfd	Lot to say about Union
124	" N Clark	Bedr	Jd Union
125	" H Cleverley	"	Do

Statement		Remarks

on Sunday at Meeting   A.C.   D⁴ 25.7.01   Paid Weeks wages.

A C   D⁴ 25.7.01   Paid Weeks wages.

Quietly agitating others   A.C   D⁴ 25 VII   Paid Week's Wages

A.C   D⁴ 25 VII   Paid Week's wages

&   A C   D⁴ 25 VII   Paid Week's wages

Union to Dr Priest.

If quiet they would not be stopped

for attending meeting at Bradford

___

Drunkard. ✓   Not Joined says Ashcroft

Others that should not teach new hands, than there   D⁴ 27 VII   Paid Week's Wages

D⁴ 27 VII   Pd Weeks Wages

D⁴ 26 VII   Paid Weeks wages

D⁴ 26 VII   Paid Weeks wages

to dismissed hands: "Good Old Brabham"   D⁴ 27 VII   Pd Weeks Wages

that he has Joined the Union   D⁴ 27 VII   Pd Weeks Wages

D⁴ 27 VII   Pd Weeks Wages

D⁴ 27 VII   Pd Weeks Wages

D⁴ 27 VII   Pd Weeks Wages

instigation of Dinner Hand   D⁴ 27 VII   Pd Weeks Wages

D⁴ 27 VII   Pd Weeks Wages

D⁴ 27 VII   Pd Weeks Wages

Staple Hill gave information
that they were at Meeting Journal

Do

Do

in Shepherds Hall So Member E. P.

Sunday Dr   Told Castle   E. P.

Do   Do   E. P.

Do   E. P.

E. P.

E P

E P

- Say U. will have its way later E. P.

at Bed⁴ meeting (Chorley)   D⁴ 27 VII   Pd Weeks Wages

Do   D⁴ 27 VII   Pd Weeks Wages

No	Name	Line	Statement
126	Driver Murphy	Sta. Hot.	With Hotheads in my presence
127	Dri. A. W. White	Bro Hot	Do
128	Con. G. Weston	Sup. Red	Do
129	Driver Parsons	Hot.	Do
130	„ Farnham	Hot.	Do
131	Con. Burge	Hot	Do
131	„ A Smith	Hot.	Do
132	„ J. Cunningham.	Cn. Red	Joined Union
133	Driver T. Sansford	Kn.	Off duty. At meeting Kn...
	Con Leek	Hot	At meeting Sunday

Sources

Primary sources

Trade union records from Bristol for the period 1901–1936 are very thin on the ground and I have not been able to find any with direct relevance to the struggles of the tramway workers. The national records of the National Union of Gas Workers and General Labourers are held at the Working Class Movement Library in Manchester, but there is a gap in the archive for 1901. The local press in Bristol, including the Western Daily Press and the Bristol Times and Mirror, carried detailed reports of the events of 1901, 1917, 1923 and 1936 which were invaluable in constructing a narrative of the trade union struggles. There were also verbatim reports of speeches by union speakers at meetings and rallies. The Bristol Archives hold the George White papers in which union leaflets were collected by the company. Other records held in this collection provide an insight into the financial affairs and the shareholdings of the Tramways' Company, along with a log-book of the 1901 dispute.

Statement	Remarks.
On 1st Sunday outside depot	
Do	
Do	
Do	)\
Do	\
Do Resides with Hatherell	
Do Resides with Hatherell	
—	

Published sources

The following published sources have been consulted:

The Bristol Omnibus Company, *The People's Carriage*, 1874–1974 (Bristol, 1974).

C. Harvey and J. Press, *Sir George White of Bristol*, 1854–1916 (Bristol Historical Association, Bristol, 1989).

A. Briggs and J. Saville (eds), *Essays in Labour History* (London, 1967).

W. Collison, *The Apostle of Free Labour* (London, 1913).

R. Kidner, 'The development of the picketing immunity, 1825–1906'. *Legal Studies*, Vol 13, 1993.

J. McNeill, *Ben Tillett* (BRHG, Bristol, 2012).

Picture Credits

Page 2—Old Market , Courtesy of Bristol Evening Post.

Page 6—Sir George White, from *The People's Carriage*, 1874-1974.

Page 8—Advertisement 1st August 1901, Bristol Libraries, newspaper collection.

Page 12—Company's logbook of the 1901, Bristol Archives, Sir George White papers, 35810.

Page 15—Brislington tramway depot drawn by Samuel Loxton, Courtesy of Bristol Libraries.

Page 16—Advertisement 7th August, Bristol Libraries, newspaper collection.

Page 18—Strikebreakers bed down for the night, Know Your Place, kypwest.org.uk.

Page 21—Advert 16th August, Bristol Libraries, newspaper collection.

Page 24—Recruiting leaflet, Bristol Archives, Sir George White papers, 35810.

Page 25—Tram on the Bedminster and Ashton Vale line, Courtesy of *Bristol Evening Post.*

Page 26—Handbill for a rally of tramway workers, Bristol Archives, Sir George White papers, 35810.

Page 27—Transport and General Workers Union leaflet, Bristol Archives, Sir George White papers, 35810.

Page 28—Tramways Company 'Notice to Staff', Bristol Archives, Sir George White papers, 35810.

Pages 30–39—Log book, Bristol Archives, Sir George White papers, 35810.

Acknowledgements

I would like to thank the following people for their help with my research. Firstly, the staff of the Bristol Central Library and those at the Bristol Archives for assisting me to access local newspapers and the George White papers. My thanks are also due to Professor Lois Bibbings for helping me to gain access to the University of Bristol library. My friend Colin Thomas has been an excellent sounding board for my ideas and has offered many useful comments on the text. Throughout the writing process Richard Musgrove of the Bristol Radical History Group has given much help and guidance on the technical aspects of the publishing process and has been especially helpful in finding many of the illustrations used in this pamphlet.

The fight for union rights

In the early twentieth century, workers could be sacked by their employer with impunity simply because they had joined a trade union.

Such was the situation for those who worked on Bristol's trams. In *Trouble on the Trams*, Rob Whitfield recounts how the drivers and conductors fought back when nearly one hundred of their number were dismissed in 1901.

Using contemporary newspaper reports and the company's own records, he details this dispute and those that were to follow subsequently, until union recognition was finally achieved over three decades later.

ISBN 978-1-91152...

£3

9 781911 522